Women 2 Women

I0484303

A Communication Guide for Business

Foreword

We have all experienced some type of communication barrier. In this tool, this guide will help you to become more effective in your communicating. There have been leaders, bosses, and entrepreneurs whom have had issues in presenting a positive communicating for success.

This guide will help you to communicate more thorough and effectively in your business, social affairs and career.

ISBN-13:

978-1505812121

ISBN-10:

1505812127

Copyright © 2015 by Diane Winbush

Open Up

How can we as women become more of a support to each other than a hindrance? Why do women have poor communication skills of assisting others for business? Have you encountered trying to communicate with another woman for business and it seems as if you can't get her to communicate? Sometimes individuals may act out of fear in a business or a career. They may be new to the area, or new to a business setting.

I can remember when beginning our business that this was a huge factor for me. My networking was out the window. I can remember being invited to a networking event and I entered the room and sat down. This should be prohibited in a networking event.

The purpose of a networking venue set up is to engage, collaborate, and share tips, tools, business cards, and information regarding your business.

This was my first real live networking event where communication was a huge factor.

I learned after this event that I needed to get my mouth into gear for business.

Besides; who will know that our businesses exist unless we market our business. The best way to market your business is to open your mouth.

I have always been a particularly shy girl and woman. But in order for me to see success in my business I knew that I would have to ditch the "quiet shell" type of mentality. By opening my mouth, our clients knew that we were now opened for business.

Communication is the aid of everyday life. Good communication is important for the daily operation of the company. Not having the communication skills which you need for business can ruin the exterior and interior of your business.

Why Do Women fail to Communicate?

Women have some issues when it comes to communicating with each other. When building a business, it takes a lot of time, restless nights, and lots of challenges will come.

Good women have a tendency of recapping all of the sweat and tears in which it took for them to get to where they are. Once someone comes in to ask them of their expertise or business help; we freeze up.

Why? Because, we as women are less reluctant to turn over all of our sweat and tears of the business to another woman. We don't like to share it with other women as a free tool or commodity.

I can remember starting out and it was really hard for us. There was no one to give us the answers on starting a business, nor did I know who to contact.

So I began to network with others by attending conferences, events, and seminars of how it worked and how our business could be more effective.

I can remember feeling like the "new kid on the block" and that it was going to take me a while to grow. But as I grew I did encounter some women who wanted to retrieve information from me without putting in any hard work themselves.

Guess what? I still had to communicate. I didn't give them any part of the business as far as information. But I had to communicate with them in a strategic way where I didn't offend them.

One day this lady whom we will call Judy, contacted me for advice. I didn't know Judy, but Judy found my information through a database.

Judy states that she had an herbal business and she needed information on how to grow her business. Well I knew that our relationship wouldn't be compatible because I wasn't in the herbal business and I felt that she was prying for information. The conversation confused me so that I had to sever the call.

Judy wasn't actually seeking my expertise; she was seeking how she could prosper from me.

You will know who and how to communicate when it comes to other women. I have never understood the factor as to why women love to utilize the "sly fox" mechanism to excel in their business. The best way to ask for help is just ask for help.

Judy didn't receive what she was set out to do. A healthy communication with another woman in business or social impact will be that the other woman isn't out for personal gain from you but that they are really in need for help and assistance.

You will know whom to share your expertise with. You will feel the hunger from the other party. How will you know? You will sense it through your woman's intuition. It will tell you.

Another example I would like to share another success story in communicating. We host a radio talk show online, I contacted a social media expert on getting more guests for my show.

 She was in the business as a radio host as well. This didn't prevent her from assisting me with her clients. She forwarded me women and more women as guests. She flooded my account with many referrals. The women were successful entrepreneurs and successors.

This was a happy ending for the both of us. She was a previous guest on my show and she returned the favor back for giving me her clients list. This is how women ought to relate to each other in business. Communicating from women 2 women will be your best option. For success in business.

How to Communicate

As the old saying goes "There is a way to do anything". Have you experienced other women such as your boss, your colleague or a personal friend communicating with anger and harshness?

This is a bad communication skill. Sometimes women respond from anger, their emotions, and their past hurts. This is why we need to ask for help in our communication. How can one receive help in this area?

Well, women need to pray daily. And yes I did say

P-R-A-Y. As this is also an effective tool in a role for business. I wouldn't want to find out that one of my staff left the business due to how I responded to him or her.

This was another area in which I could have used some training in years earlier. I had to learn and surround myself with other women whom responded to others in a calm and non-rational manner.

In my first planned event, the director of the venue had to counsel me on some things and how to handle the attendants. She gave me advice on how to receive more attendants in the area and how I needed to respond to them through my advertising and marketing strategies.

Of course, I just knew that I was doing it right all along. But you know how we can become as women; we think we know everything. The event was coming to a close and I exited the venue; I began to take her advice. People respond to you according to how you respond to them.

Do we take our authority and abuse it when communicating? Do we as women, leave our home with a chip on our shoulders and bring the issue to work?

These keys are important.

If we operate in these phases, then the same issue will return to us. Remember the Biblical term; "Do unto others as you would have them do unto you." We can concur the same issues as we have inflicted on someone else. I have learned that life has a way of boomeranging itself.

Communicating On Social Media

Now this should spark your attention! When I joined social media; I just knew that this would be a great communication forum. Not all the time.

You can experience rants of communication from other women. Some women utilize the strangest pitches on how to communicate if they desire to do business with you.

For example: A business owner whom we will call Martha; wanted to do business, but what Martha did was very un-professional and bias.

She posted a comment in regards to a grammar error. Instead of Martha in boxing me privately she posted it openly and it wasn't funny at all.

This stemmed from her not having the correct communication skills on how to communicate with other women.

If you need to market/advertise/ or brand your business; you don't need to utilize a negative pitch to get it done.

Social media is formed to build, network, and advertise your business and not destruct others through criticism. I previously wrote a blog post on LinkedIn entitled constructive and destructive criticism.

 I wrote the blog after I had posted another blog entitled; "Women what's in your purse?" Constructive criticism is when your comments are meaningful but correct.

 You may have a need to correct someone, but in a professional manner. Destructive criticism is when your comments are hurtful, harmful, and intentional. So which will receive the best outcome. It will be the constructive criticism of course.

Social media wasn't and isn't meant for badgering.

Review

Fill in The Blanks

Destructive and _____ criticism

Do women abuse their_____

 Women can respond out of _____

Open your_____

There is a way to do_____

A Lesson in _____

Successful Communication

How to have success in your communication is start with the success in you.

People can grasp a better you and it enables to resolve issues more effectively.

Effective communication can improve relationships at home, work and in social situations by deepening your connections to others.

Improving networking, teamwork, decision making, and problem solving are all ways if how a good communication can result invite allows you to communicate even negative or difficult messages without creating conflict or destroying trust.

Here are more tips and resources in which I would like to share with you:

 # Listening

#Focus totally on what is being said to you

#Avoid interrupting

#Avoid being judgmental

#Show your interest and concerns

#Practice observing others

#Be cautious of individual differences

#Empathize with others

#Be transparent

#Communicate clearly and effectively

#Agree to Disagree

#Look for some humor in the situation

#Bring your senses to the table

We have shared with you tons of information, tools, and resources on how women can communicate with each other. Having barriers is just one way of not being transparent in a conversation.

We need to utilize these tools to have a healthy and successful business through our communication practices.

Networking Checklist

_____ Business Cards

_____ Professional Attire

_____ Business Plan (Niche)

_____ Smiles

_____ Exchange contact information

_____ Referrals for other attendants

_____ Follow Up with Business referrals

_____ Follow Up with Business Contacts

_____ Check business cards for information accuracy

Business Journal

How will you be more supportive to other women?

_____

_____

_____

_____

_____

_____

_____

_____

_____

_____

_____

_____

_____

_____

_____

_____

How can women count on you for support?

_____

_____

_____

_____

_____

_____

_____

_____

_____

_____

_____

_____

_____

_____

_____

_____

Today; women can expect from me

_____

_____

_____

_____

_____

_____

_____

_____

_____

_____

_____

_____

_____

_____

_____

_____

_____

My business can build other women because

_____

_____

_____

_____

_____

_____

_____

_____

_____

_____

_____

_____

_____

_____

_____

My support of resources isn't given grudgingly because

_____

_____

_____

_____

_____

_____

_____

_____

_____

_____

_____

_____

_____

_____

_____

_____

Do I desire to see other women excel for business?
Why?

_____

_____

_____

_____

_____

_____

_____

_____

_____

_____

_____

_____

_____

_____

_____

Am I fearful in helping other women build their brand?

_____

_____

_____

_____

_____

_____

_____

_____

_____

_____

_____

_____

_____

_____

Notes

www.ingramcontent.com/pod-product-compliance
Lightning Source LLC
Chambersburg PA
CBHW050353180526
45159CB00005B/2005